Co
With Notation

PIANO

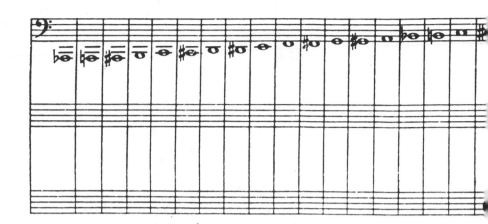

VIOLIN

Bb CLARINET

SOPRANO SAXOPHONE
(Bb)

ALTO SAXOPHONE
(Eb)

C MELODY SAXOPHONE

TENOR SAXOPHONE
(Bb)

BARITONE SAXOPHONE
(Eb)

BASS SAXOPHONE
(Bb)

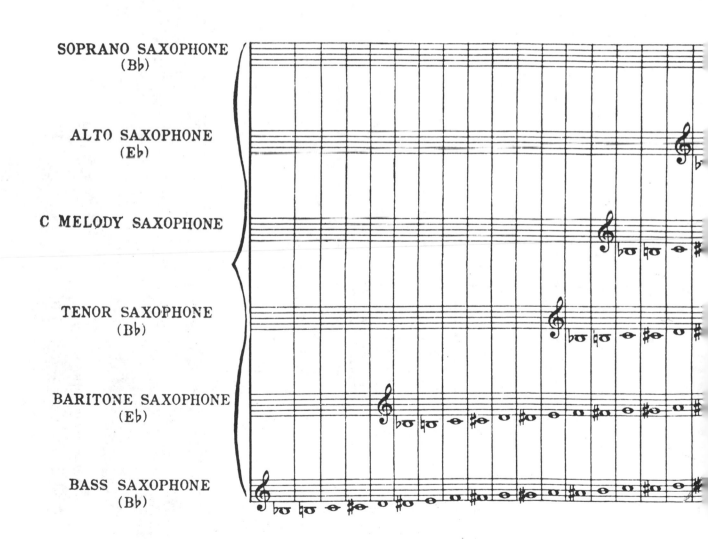

	B♮	C	C♯ or D♭	D♮	D♯ or E♭	E♮	F

LEFT HAND
- Fore finger .... D♯
- .... D
- Middle finger .... F
- Ring finger ....

B - C trill

RIGHT HAND
- Fore finger ....
- Middle finger ....
- Ring finger ....
- Little finger ....

bove 𝄞 see "Top Tones for the Saxophone"

her, Published by Carl Fischer, Inc., N.Y.

OMPLETE SCALE FOR ALL SAXOPHONE
by
SIGURD M. RASCHER

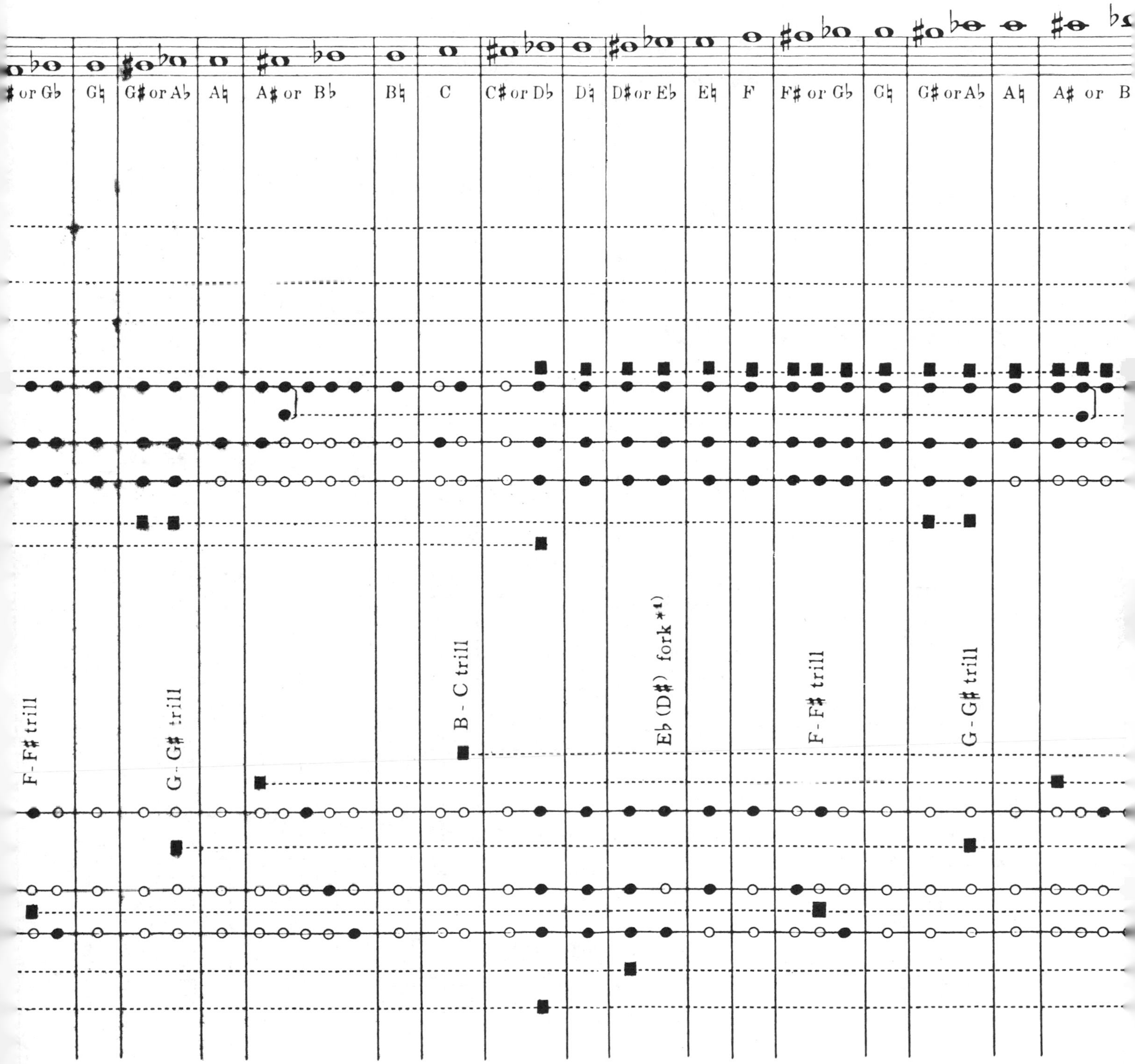

or G♭	G♮	G♯ or A♭	A♮	A♯ or B♭	B♮	C	C♯ or D♭	D♮	D♯ or E♭	E♮	F	F♯ or G♭	G♮	G♯ or A♭	A♮	A♯ or B

Labels within the chart:

- F - F♯ trill
- G - G♯ trill
- B - C trill
- E♭ (D♯) fork *¹)
- F - F♯ trill
- G - G♯ trill

or "E flat Fork"

*²) For fingerings

by S. M. Ra

CARL FISCHER
mplete Table of all Saxophones
nd Compass as compared with Piano, Violin and Bb Clarinet

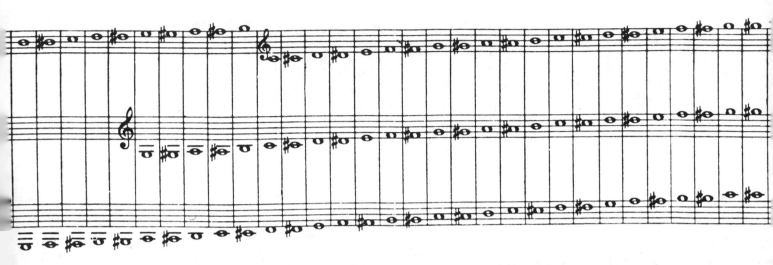

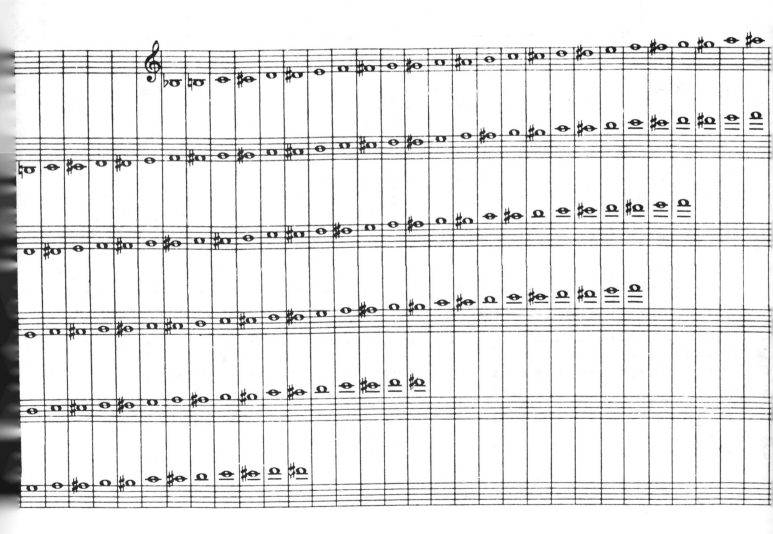

The Saxophone in the Orchestra

Practical Hints regarding Transposition and Adaptation of Orchestra Parts to suit the Requirements, Character and Peculiarities of the differently pitched Saxophones.

SAXOPHONES, the tonal quality of which have long since made them practically indispensable for bands, are gradually being introduced with growing favor into smaller orchestras and it seems only a question of time when they will be included in the regular wind section of every orchestra, large or small

Saxophones are treble clef (𝄞) instruments and the fingering on all of them is the same.

THE SOPRANO, can play the part of Bb Clarinet or Cornet; if these parts are written for A Clarinet or Cornet they should be played one half-tone lower than written. Oboe, Flute and Violin parts can also be used, but must be read and played one tone higher

THE ALTO, can play Cello, Bassoon and Trombone parts by ignoring the bass clef and substituting the treble clef. These parts are played one octave lower than written, as far as possible and when the part runs too low it should be played as written.

Notice should be taken that in substituting the treble for the bass clef the part will naturally appear in a different key. For instance:- When the Cello, Trombone or Bassoon parts are written in C, the Saxophone will have to play in A. The following will illustrate this point in several different ways:-

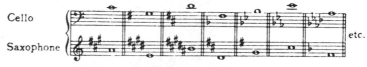

The Alto is also well suited to take the part of the Viola. To read the Viola part properly, ignore the alto clef(𝄡), and substitute the treble clef and read and play the part one tone lower than written. The same change of keys as in the case of the Cello must be observed.

THE C MELODY is the instrument best adapted for use in the orchestra, as it requires no transposition and is pitched in the same key as all the orchestra instruments with the exception of Clarinet, Cornet and Horns. The Melody Saxophone is best suited to take the Cello part which must be read and played in the bass clef (𝄢) and with no other transposition necessary. When the part runs into the tenor clef (𝄐) substitute the treble clef, and play the notes one tone lower than written. Whenever the Cello part should run into the treble clef (𝄞) play that part one octave higher than written, the same to be observed when any other part, in that clef, (such as Violin, Flute and Oboe) is to be played. Bassoon and Trombone parts are played in the identical way as Cello parts.

THE Bb TENOR can play the same parts as the Soprano but should play those parts an octave higher than written. In reality the Tenor is better adapted to play the parts of Cello, Bassoon or Trombone; these should be read and played in the bass clef (𝄢), one tone higher, or can be played four tones lower by reading them in the treble clef (𝄞). (See bass line in Complete Table).

THE BARITONE can play the part of Cello, Bassoon, Trombone and String Bass by ignoring the bass (𝄢), and substituting the treble clef (𝄞); the same changes of key as indicated in the example for Cello and Alto Saxophone must be observed.

THE BASS is exclusively used for the String Bass part. The Bb Tuba part in treble clef (𝄞) can also be played without making any alterations. But in order to use the String Bass part read and play in the bass clef (𝄢), one tone higher, changing the key accordingly. (See bass line in Complete Table).

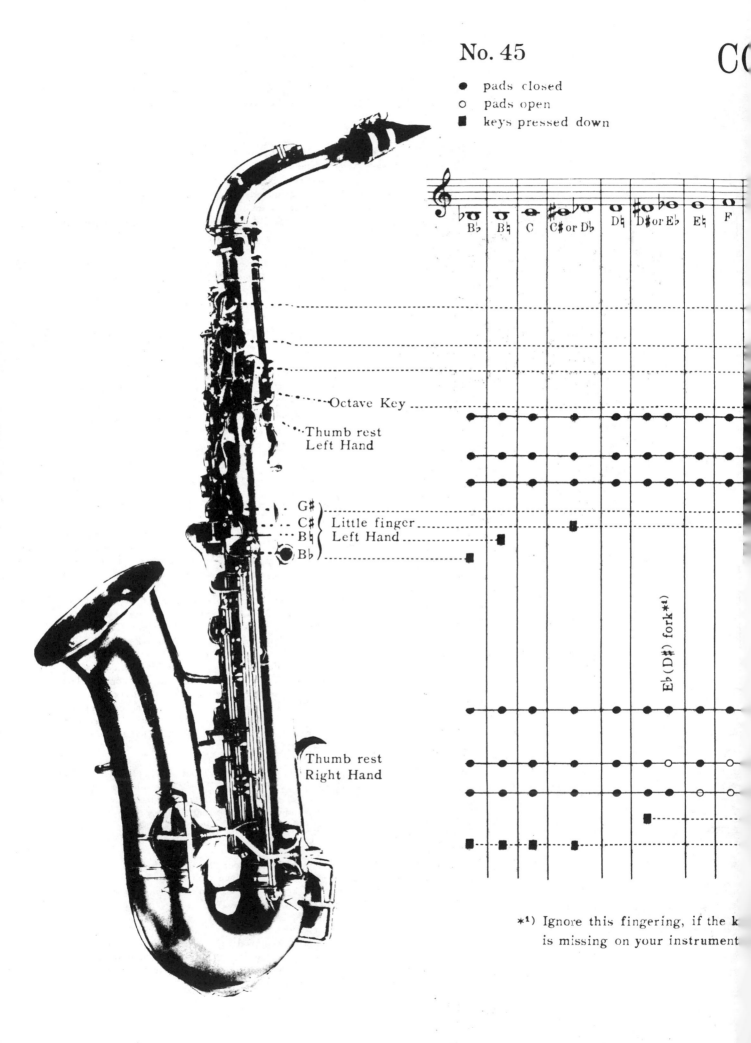

*1) Ignore this fingering, if the k
is missing on your instrument

Foundation to SAXOPHONE PLAYING

AN ELEMENTARY METHOD

New and Revised Edition

by

BEN VEREECKEN

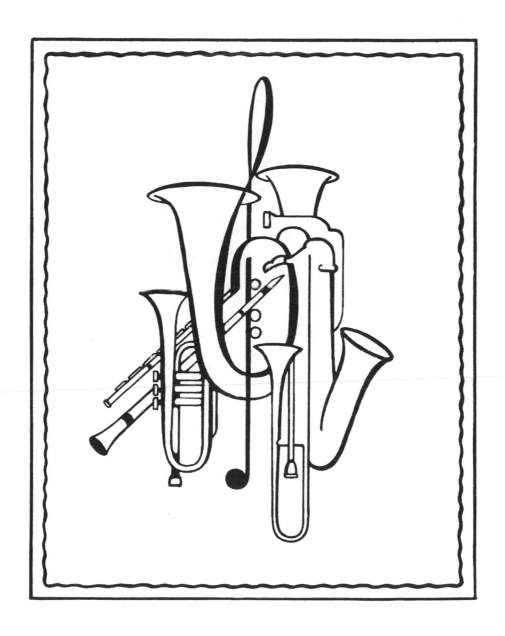

CARL FISCHER®

65 Bleecker Street, New York, NY 10012

O224

ISBN 0-8258-3355-8

Contents

Introduction

The need of an elementary method for self-instruction, has prompted me to write this book. To be sure, there are several other methods for Saxophone, but none of them can be used by beginners, without the aid of a teacher.

It must be borne in mind that many students are not within reach of competent instructors, and must depend to a large extent upon self-instruction. Therefore, in order to accomplish any satisfactory results, each exercise and solo must be thoroughly explained. In this work, there is an explanation to everything, and thus the student acquires a thorough knowledge of the rudiments of music, and of his instrument, from the very outset. It should be remembered also that in most instances, even when the student was fortunate enough to secure a teacher, many special lessons had to be given first, in order to prepare him for the method, as it was found that most of the good methods published did not contain exercises which the beginner could attempt to play. With this book, the prospective player, who has never before had a Saxophone in his hands, can immediately take up the first lesson, after he has read the preliminary explanations.

Through my years of experience as teacher and performer, I have become familiar with the requirements of beginners, and it is this practical knowledge that has given me the inspiration to write this book. The work embraces all the points that I, through personal experience have found to be of benefit to the pupil.

The exercises are mostly short, so as not to tire the player. They also progress very systematically. Every exercise is original and cannot be found in any other book. The recreations are pleasing and melodious, and the fifty studies in the style of preludes are interesting and instructive. At the rear of the book will be found some brilliant solos and fantasies.

The student who has mastered these studies and profited by all the other advice and suggestions given will have a good and solid foundation upon which to build, and there is no reason why he should not become a fine performer.

It has been my aim to make this book valuable to both pupil and teacher, particularly to the pupil who is not fortunate enough to be within reach of a competent instructor, and must content himself with self-instruction.

THE AUTHOR.

The Saxophone

The Saxophone was invented about the year 1845 by Adolphe Sax, a Belgian, living in Paris, France, who named it after himself.

Originally the Saxophone was very cumbersome and not easy to manipulate, but it has been improved to such an extent within recent years that the most difficult passages may now be executed with comparative ease and little practice. It is now recognized as an indispensible instrument in both brass and reed bands, and has also found a place in the orchestra.

The Saxophone family consists of the Soprano in Bb,—the Alto in Eb,—the Melody Tenor in C,—the Tenor in Bb,—the Baritone in Eb, and the Bass in Bb,—all of which are used with brilliant effect.

The Alto Saxophone is the principal instrument. If two are used they should be Alto and Tenor,—then adding Baritone.

The tonal quality of the Saxophone is very smooth and pleasing to the ear, and its mechanism permits of very brilliant execution.

Position of the Body

The head and body must be kept erect, the weight of the body resting on the right leg, while the left foot should be a little advanced. In sitting, the position in which the instrument is held is just the same.

Manner of Holding the Saxophone

A strap which is attached to the instrument and placed around the neck of the player, enables him to hold it with comfort and steadiness. Such a strap is used on all the models except the Soprano (Clarinet Model).

The right hand is placed at the lower end of the instrument, and the thumb under the hook, which aids in balancing it.

The left hand is placed at the upper part, the thumb on the button below the octave key.

The instrument hangs toward the right just about where the thumb of the right hand touches the vest pocket (Alto Saxophone). The other Saxophones must be held in the same position although the greater size of the instruments might change the position of both arms slightly.

Adjusting the Reed

The reed must be placed on the flat of the mouthpiece so that the tapered edge comes about even with the top end of the mouthpiece. It must be fastened securely at the lower end with the ligature.

Position of the Mouthpiece

The mouthpiece, with the reed underneath, is held between the lips and a little less than half of its curved part is covered.

Draw the lower lip easily over the teeth so that the reed does not touch the teeth. The upper teeth are applied to the mouthpiece.

To Produce the Tone

Keep the lips around the mouthpiece so that it is impossible for any air to escape through the corners of the mouth. Then bring the point of the tongue to the end of the reed, where it is easiest to press it against the mouthpiece. Draw the tongue back sharply allowing the breath to escape into the mouthpiece with a "T" effect.

These movements of the tongue constitute what is called "Tonguing."

The tonguing must be executed vigorously so as to set the column of air into immediate vibration.

Tuning

Before starting to play, always warm up the instrument by blowing your warm breath through it, or by preluding a little if possible. Heat and cold have opposite effects on the Saxophone. When cold, the instrument is flat and when warm it becomes sharp.

The pitch can be regulated to a certain degree by pulling out the mouthpiece when too sharp, and pushing it in further when too flat.

Too much pressure on the reed will make the pitch too sharp, while using too little pressure will create the opposite effect, and the quality of tone will be harsh and disagreeable.

Many good instruments are played out of tune in this way. If the ear is carefully trained, the performer will have little difficulty in playing well in tune.

Care should be taken to avoid swelling of the cheeks as this not only looks bad but impairs the quality of tone and surety of attack. It would be advisable to stand before a mirror occasionally when practicing in order to correct any faulty position, and so that any contortions of the face may be avoided.

Care of the Instrument

Be careful to keep your instrument clean. A small soft brush is very useful for removing dust from between the keys.

If the pads should get wet, they should be dried immediately with a cloth.

Dust or dampness harden the pads and clog the openings, preventing proper covering of the holes.

When the pads become hard and stiff they should be replaced with new ones.

The springs should be oiled occasionally.

Before Playing

Be sure that your reed is not too stiff or too soft. If too stiff, it not only produces a dry and harsh tone, but is also injurious to the player. If too soft, the tone will be thick and unnatural. This defect is particularly noticeable in the lower and higher registers. The lower notes will not respond readily except with exertion, indicating that your reed is too hard, and when the higher notes sound thin and unnatural and are unresponsive, it is generally because the reed is too soft. A reed which answers both purposes must be used.

Before applying the reed to the mouthpiece, it should be moistened or wet at the thinner end. See that it is not curved as that would stop the tone production.

To straighten a reed, moisten it, then place the curved part on a flat surface pressing it there with your thumb for a few seconds.

After Playing

Remove the reed and dry it. Then dry and clean the saliva from the mouthpiece. Any moisture on the keys or pads should also be removed with a soft cloth.

It is advisable to keep the reed removed from the mouthpiece until it is to be used again.

The reed should be placed in a box, preferably against a piece of glass. In this manner it will keep straight.

How to Practice

Practice regularly each day, if possible.

Do not attempt too much at first and do not get discouraged if the first studies prove tiresome and monotonous.

Play all music exactly as written.

Do not over-exert yourself when playing.

Practice in such a manner that you can play without apparent effort, and can derive pleasure from it.

Do not practice too long at one time. Too much or too strenuous practice is as harmful as too little.

Listen carefully and you will hear if a tone is good or bad.

Hold your instrument steady so that it cannot move and interfere with the good quality of tone and the execution.

What to Practice

Practice whatever may be necessary and what you are not familiar with. Sustained tones should be practiced a few minutes each day before anything else. This helps to strengthen the lips and will improve the quality of tone. This is very important, as a good tone is the performer's most valuable asset.

Do not fail to practice all sorts of exercises and scales.

In striking tones, especially in rapid execution, the fingers and the tongue must work simultaneously.

Give particular attention to the quality of tone, also to style of performance and to phrasing.

Avoid the "tremolo" or "vibrato" style of playing. See that your tone is absolutely clear and pure.

Transposition

Learn to transpose. This is a positive necessity for professionals and is very convenient and desirable for amateurs. It should not be studied however, until the pupil has a fair knowledge of the rudiments of music and is beyond the first stages of playing.

It is very essential that the performer who expects to play in orchestra, should have knowledge of the Bass Clef, the Tenor Clef and the Treble Clef, which are the three principal ones.

With a knowledge of the Treble and Bass, all the other Clefs are easily acquired, and transposition becomes very simple and easy.

SIGNS MOST FREQUENTLY USED.

• A Dot placed after a note or rest prolongs its value by half. ♩· would be the same as ♩♪ A second or third dot prolongs the time value of the dot immediately preceding it by half. ♩··· would be the same as ♩♪♫

— *Tenuto.* This line when placed over or, under a note signifies that the tone should be well sustained, for its full value.

⌢ or ⌣ *Hold* or *Pause,* placed over or under a note or rest indicates an indefinite prolongation of its time value, at the performer's discretion.

𝄆𝄇 *Repeat.* This sign signifies that the division between the dotted double bars is to be repeated.

❜ *Breathing mark.* A sign which indicates where breath may be taken.

⌢ *Slur* or *Tie.* This sign indicates that when two or more notes are joined by it, they are to be played in a smooth and connected manner. (Legato.) If the notes so joined are on the same degree of the staff they are held over as one note.

⟨ *Crescendo,* increasing in loudness, by degrees.

⟩ *Decrescendo,* growing softer by degrees.

∧ *Sforzato,* marked or sudden emphasis.

〰 *tr Trill,* the rapid alternation of a principal note with a higher auxiliary, (major or minor second above).

∾ *Turn* or *Grupetto,* a melodic grace consisting in what may be termed the typical form (the direct turn), of four notes, a principal note (twice struck) with its higher and lower auxiliary (the major and minor second above and below, each struck once.)

M.M. ♩=60 *Metronome mark,* a mark often set at the beginning of a composition for exactly indicating its tempo. The ♩=60 means, that the time value of one quarter note is equal to one pendulum-beat with the slider set at 60. With the slider set at 60, the pendulum makes one beat per second. M. M. actually stands for "Maelzel's Metronome," named after its inventor, Maelzel, of Vienna. The Metronome is much used by beginners and students, for learning to play strictly in time and in timing their practice.

f — *Forte,* means loud, strong.

ff — *Fortissimo,* means very loud.

mf — *Mezzo forte,* half loud.

p — *Piano,* soft.

pp — *Pianissimo,* very soft.

D.C. — *Da Capo,* from the beginning.

D.S. — *Dal Segno,* repeat from the sign.

For other signs, etc. see Coon's Standard Pocket Dictionary Musical Terms.

19911 102 (17513)

Rudiments of Music.

Music is the art of combining sounds in a manner agreeable to the ear.

It is divided into two parts:— Melody and Harmony.

Melody is a combination of sounds which, by their elevation, duration and succession, serve to form a tune.

Harmony is another combination of sounds which, by their spontaneous union, serve to form chords.

The Signs used to represent sound are called notes.

The five lines upon which notes are written are called the Staff.

The Staff consists of five lines and four spaces.

Extra lines are used above and below the staff. They are called ledger lines.

Seven letters of the alphabet are used to designate the notes; they are, C-D-E-F-G-A-B.

At the beginning of each line of music you will find the clef sign ($\mathsubstack{}$)

The Clef is used to determine the position and pitch of the scale. This clef is called the G or Treble clef. It shows where G is thereby giving place to the other notes. The sign crosses the second line "G" four times.

There are other clefs, but they are not used

There are seven natural tones in Music, to which is added an eighth tone, which, however, is only a repetition of the first tone an octave higher.

When the notes are written in the Treble Clef, the names of the lines and spaces are as follows:—

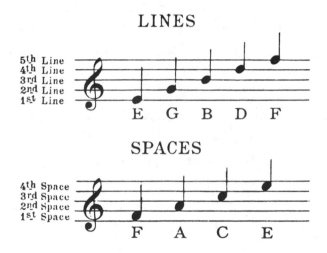

The notes that can be written on the staff are not enough to enable us to indicate all the tones that are within the range and compass of the Saxophone. For this reason, it becomes necessary to go beyond the staff, and use what are termed "Ledger Lines and Spaces."

LEDGER LINES

The distance between two notes is called "interval."

NOTES

There are seven characters which determine the value of notes.

o whole note — 4 beats or counts.

𝅗𝅥 half note — 2 beats or counts.

♩ quarter note — 1 beat or count.

♪ eighth note — $\frac{1}{2}$ beat.

𝅘𝅥𝅯 sixteenth note —

𝅘𝅥𝅰 thirty second note —

𝅘𝅥𝅱 sixty-fourth note —

RESTS

There are seven characters that denote the value of rests,

▬ whole rest — 4 beats or counts

▬ half rest — 2 beats or counts.

𝄽 quarter rest — 1 beat or count.

𝄾 eighth rest — $\frac{1}{2}$ beat or count.

𝄿 sixteenth rest —

𝅀 thirty second rest —

𝅁 sixty-fourth rest —

A Rest is a character used to indicate silence, or a temporary suspension of sounds.

SHARPS, FLATS, NATURALS ETC.

The Sharp (♯) raises the note half a tone.

The Flat (♭) lowers the note half a tone.

The Natural (♮) restores the note which has been changed by the ♯ or ♭ to its former position.

The Double Sharp (𝄪) raises a note a half tone higher than the simple (♯) would raise it. In other words, it raises the note a whole tone.

The Double Flat (♭♭)lowers a note a half tone lower than the simple ♭ would lower it,— in other words, a whole tone.

Always after the Clef, we must look for the Signature, or key, in which we are to play.

The word Signature signifies a certain number of sharps or flats placed immediately after the clef.

Either sharps or flats found after the Clef as Signature, influence the notes placed on the same degree, or at the upper or lower octave, during the whole of a piece of music, unless a natural comes accidentally to suspend their effect.

If a sharp or flat is written in any bar without being designated at the beginning (in the Signature), such sharp or flat is called an "Accidental", and holds good only for the bar in which it is written. If this sign is to be contradicted, in said bar, a"natural" must be placed before the note in question.

MEASURES AND BARS

Musical Composition is divided into equal portions,— called Measures or Bars, by short lines drawn across the staff which are also called Bars.

A double Bar is placed at the end of each strain of music.

Measures are divided into equal parts called "beats".

All music does not begin with a perfect or full bar. The first bar may be imperfect and contain what is known as "start notes". There may be one or more of such start notes. However, the first and last bars of a strain, or of a complete piece, must together form a full bar.

TIME MARKS

Immediately after the signature comes the Time Mark.

There are various kinds of time marks, but those most frequently used are, $\frac{4}{4}$-$\frac{3}{4}$-$\frac{2}{4}$ and $\frac{6}{8}$.

There are many other time marks, such as, $\frac{2}{2}$-$\frac{3}{2}$-$\frac{6}{4}$-$\frac{5}{4}$-$\frac{3}{8}$-$\frac{9}{8}$-$\frac{12}{8}$, etc., etc., but in this book, only the simpler forms will be used.

The upper figure (numerator) indicates the number of notes of a given kind in the measure.

The lower figure (denominator) shows the kind of notes, taken as the unit of measure.

Time refers to the number of beats to the measure.

Tempo indicates the rapidity of the beats.

The two are often confounded.

19911- 102 (17513)

After having carefully studied the chart and picture of the Saxophone, you will be acquainted with the letters and figures.

The letters A, B, C indicate the pads to be manipulated with the first (fore), second (middle) and third (ring) finger of the left hand.

The letters D, E, F indicate the pads to be manipulated with the first (fore), second (middle) and third (ring) finger of the right hand respectively; or 1, 2, 3, for left, and 4, 5, 6 for right hand.

The little fingers shall be indicated whenever they are to be used

The Roman numbers indicate the keys.

The thumb of the left hand is placed on the button below the octave key (XII), and must not come in contact with any keys while playing in the lower register.

The fingers are held above their corresponding pads.

The thumb of the right hand is held under the hook at the lower part of the instrument.

The First lesson starts the pupil with the easier notes, and gradually reaches the lower ones which are rather difficult for beginners.

STRIKING THE TONES AND COUNTING THE TIME

Always bear in mind that time is the most important factor in music. Without time there is no real music. Endeavor from the very beginning to count mentally and play in proper tempo.

Do not count or keep time by moving the body or the feet. That is a very bad habit.

Listen to your playing, and think as you play.

It is essential to give all notes and rests their proper time value.

Attack each note properly, giving the same volume of air.

Avoid letting the tone tremble by the loosening of the lips.

Have your strap adjusted so that the mouthpiece reaches the mouth easily.

First Lesson

The first lesson is for the left hand.

These and following lessons are written in common or 4/4 time. All the notes are whole notes, and all the rests are whole rests. Count four even beats for each note and four even beats for each rest.

Count evenly and not too quickly.

Remember that in all music the rests are just as important as the notes.

The first lessons will be marked until the student has become familiar with the different notes, rests, etc.

Start this lesson by counting 1, 2, 3, 4 and keep on counting (mentally) until the end.

In the second measure, strike your note (G) and hold same until you have again counted "four". Execute the following measures in a similar manner.

Second Lesson

In the second lesson the left and right hands are used.

Start again by counting 1, 2, 3, 4. The second measure is played as in the first lesson. In the fourth measure, in order to play F, add the first finger of the right hand on pad D, and continue as marked.

Third Lesson
FOR THE USE OF THE FIRST OCTAVE KEY

In case your Saxophone has only one octave key which is a late improvement, it should be manipulated as though you were using the first key, by rolling your thumb on the key without leaving the button. This key is marked on the chart "VII" and is used from D to G♯ (or A♭) inclusive.

To start the first note D in this lesson, place the fingers of both hands on their respective pads as marked, and open first octave key VII. Hold key open for every note in this lesson.

In order to produce the notes easily with the octave keys, press a little firmer on your reed with the lip.

NOTICE: The fingering of the second octave is the same as that of the first, except that the first octave key is added.

1st Lesson

ON STRIKING THE TONES AND COUNTING THE TIME

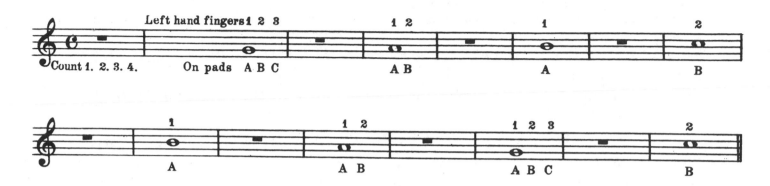

2nd Lesson

LEFT AND RIGHT HAND

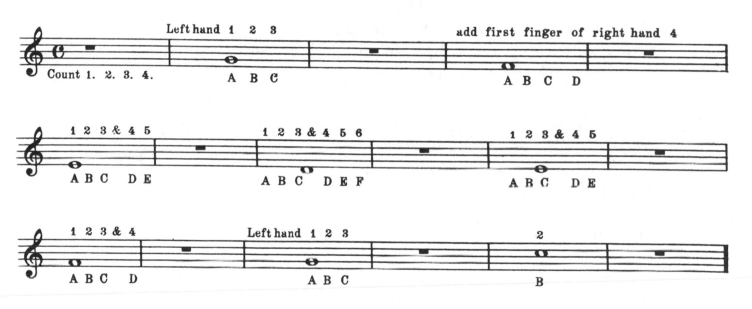

3rd Lesson

FIRST OCTAVE KEY VII

19911- 102

Fourth Lesson
THE SECOND OCTAVE KEY

The second octave key is marked in chart XII.

This key is used for all the notes above G♯. Thus beginning with

A whenever the second octave key is used, the first octave key must be released, and vice-versa

If your instrument has the single octave key, then all the notes from D up are played with that key.

This lesson is also played with the left hand, the same as the first lesson, with the additional use of the second octave key.

To use this key, roll your thumb forward until you can reach same without leaving button.

Fifth Lesson
THE TWO OCTAVES
(With addition of the low C, which is manipulated with the little finger of the right hand) See chart, Key marked "III"

In this lesson, we shall leave out the figures indicating the fingers, and just use the letters for the pads.

In playing these scales you will feel that higher notes require a little more pressure on the mouthpiece than the lower notes.

Sixth Lesson
ON WHOLE, HALF AND QUARTER NOTES

A measure, also called a bar, in common (C) or 4/4 time consists of one whole, or two halves, or four quarter notes, or their equivalent.

The bars or measures are divided by straight lines.

Attack each note properly as heretofore described, and keep the tempo correct.
Do not play one bar faster or slower than another.
The respiration marks (9) will be used for the first lessons.
We will take breath more frequently at the beginning.
Breath must be taken through the corners of the mouth.

4th Lesson
ON THE SECOND OCTAVE KEY (XII)

5th Lesson
THE TWO OCTAVES
(with addition of the low C. Key III)

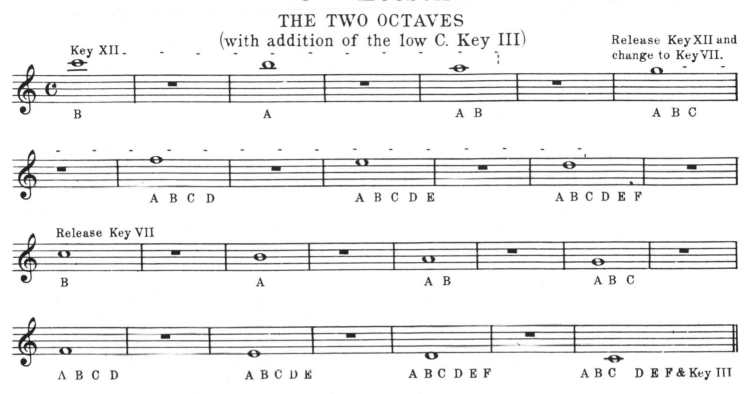

6th Lesson
ON WHOLE, HALF AND QUARTER NOTES

Seventh Lesson
THE CHROMATIC SCALE
Comprising all the keys

Figures for the fingers will now be omitted, but the letters for the pads, and figures for the keys will be used in this lesson.

Before trying to play the scale, study the chart very attentively. Afterwards, with the chart before you it will be a simple matter to find the required keys.

The Roman numbers for the keys are marked below the lines, the letters for the pads above.

Notice that whenever the little finger of either the right or left hand is used all the pads taken with the six fingers must remain closed.

The first note, Bb, which is the lowest note on the Saxophone, is made with the six fingers down, with little finger of right hand on key III, and little finger of left hand on key I B.

B♮ - - - - Shift little finger of left hand from I B to key I

C - - - - Release little finger of left hand.

C♯ or D♭ - Place little finger of hand on key II.

For the above notes, keep little finger of right hand on key III.

D♮ - - - - Release both little fingers.

D♯ or E♭ - Place little finger of right hand on key IV.

E♮ - - - - Release key IV and open pad F.

F - - - - The four first pads.

F♯ or G♭ - The three first pads and the fifth.

G♮ - - - - The three first pads.

G♯ or A♭ - The three first pads and key V with little finger of left hand.

A♮ - - - - The two first pads.

A♯ or B♭ The two first pads and key VI with third joint of first finger of the right hand.

B♮ - - - - The first pad.

C - - - - The second pad.

C♯ or D♭ - All open pads. Balance the instrument on both thumbs and the strap.

D♮ - - - - The second octave from D up, is taken just the same way as the first or lower octave with the addition of the octave key VII which is taken with the thumb of the left hand. Thus, the six pads and octave key VII.

D♯ or E♭ - The six pads, octave key and key IV with little finger of right hand.

E♮ - - - - The five first pads and octave key.

F - - - - The four first pads and octave key.

F♯ or G♭ - The three first pads, pad five and octave key.

G♮ - - - - The three first pads and octave key.

G♯ or A♭ - The three first pads, key V and octave key.

For the following notes, release the first octave key.

A♮ - - - - The two first pads and octave key. (If the Saxophone has the two octave keys, the second, marked XII must be used for this.) If only one, the single key must be kept open.

A♯ or B♭ - The first two pads, key VI and octave key.

B♮ - - - - The first pad and octave key.

C - - - - The second pad and octave key.

C♯ or D♭ - Release all pads, but retain octave key.

D♮ - - - - Key VIII and octave key.

D♯ or E♭ - Key VIII, key IX and octave key. This is the limit of the Soprano, Baritone and Bass Saxophones

E♮ - - - - Keys VIII, IX, X and octave key.

F - - - - Keys VIII, IX, X, XI and octave key.

7th Lesson

THE CHROMATIC SCALE
(Comprising all the Keys)

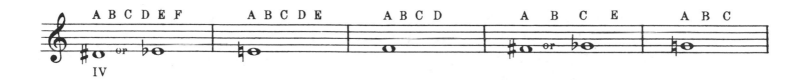

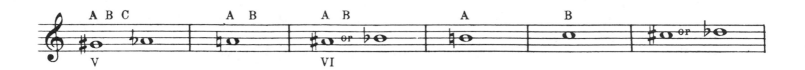

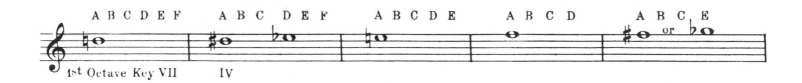

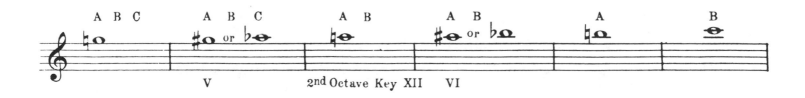

MANIPULATION OF THE EXTRA KEYS

There are different makes of Saxophones with various systems and improvements. **One** of these has three little petals (or levers) which make it possible to produce the following extra low notes:

While taking low C [musical notation] the middle finger of the right hand can be raised without changing the note, and used for any of the three petals as follows:

The first petal for B♭, the second for B♮ and the third for C♯.

These three notes are otherwise manipulated with the little finger of the left hand.

Low and middle D♯ or E♭ can be taken by moving the middle finger of right hand a little lower, which will close the pad of the third finger, leaving third and little finger free, which are otherwise used to make D♯ or E♭.

F♯ or G♭ can be produced by placing the four first fingers on their pads, using sixth finger for key XIII.

A♯ or B♭ can be taken with the first finger on pad A and fourth finger on pad D; also with first finger on pad A and Fifth finger on pad E; and with first finger on pad A and second finger on pad A^{bis}; and again with first and second fingers on pads A and B and Key VI with first finger of the right hand.

C can be taken with first finger on pad A and key VI B with second joint of the first finger of right hand.

The high E [musical notation] can be taken with the second and third finger on pads B and C respectively, leaving the first finger free to work the key which is placed above pad A.

F can be taken with the use of the same key, placing the second finger on pad B and first finger on same key, above pad A.

Other systems have most of the above extra keys with the exception of the B♭, B♮ and C♯ in lower register.

On some systems the E♭ is manipulated with the three first fingers of the left hand, and first and third of the right hand on their respective pads, leaving middle finger of right hand free.

Exercises for the use of all these extra keys will be found further in this book.

Eighth Lesson

THREE QUARTER (¾) TIME, THE DOT (·) AND TWO QUARTER ² ⁄ ₄ TIME.

(A) This exercise is in three quarter (¾) time, which means that each bar must contain the value of three quarter notes. Three beats or counts to each bar.

(B) The dot placed behind a note or rest, increases the value of the note or rest one half. A half note followed by a dot [musical notation] has the value of three quarters.

(C) This exercise is in two quarter (²⁄₄) time, which means that each bar must contain the value of two quarter notes, - two beats or counts to each bar.

(D) This is a simple melody in two - quarter time.

8th Lesson
THREE-QUARTER ($\frac{3}{4}$) TIME, THE DOT, AND TWO-QUARTER ($\frac{2}{4}$) TIME

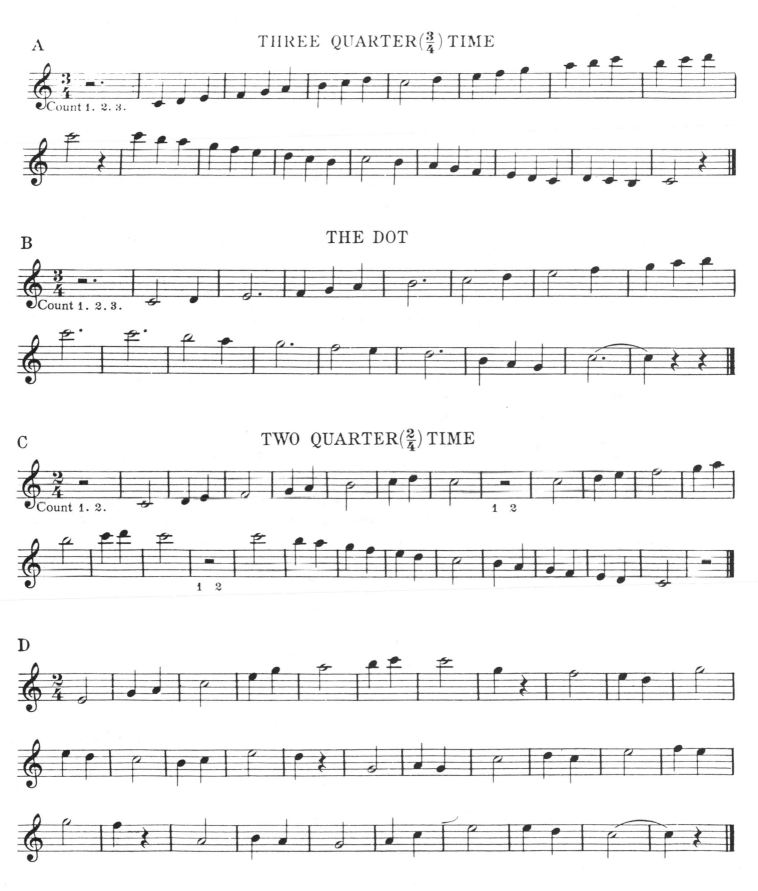

Ninth Lesson

PROGRESSIVE EXERCISES ON THE INTERVALS

This and the following few lessons are exercises on the intervals.

An interval is the distance from one tone to another.
The smallest interval in music is that of a semitone (half tone.)

A major scale contains two semitones, one from the third to the fourth and another from the seventh to the eighth degrees.

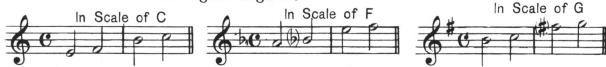

In the next few lessons, the student will find notes of different values in order to prepare him for the more progressive exercises.

The Ninth lesson. is composed of seconds
The Tenth, of thirds
The Eleventh, of fourths
The Twelfth, of fifths
The Thirteenth, of sixths
The Fourteenth, of sevenths
The Fifteenth, of eighths, which are called octaves.

Attack each note of these lessons separately and observe strict time.
Do not play one note louder than another, and pronounce the T distinctly.

9th Lesson
EXERCISES ON THE INTERVALS

10th Lesson

11th Lesson

Fourths

12th Lesson

Fifths

13th Lesson

Sixths

14th Lesson

Sevenths

15th Lesson

Octaves

Sixteenth Lesson
PROGRESSIVE EXERCISES ON ARTICULATION

These exercises are all based on the same theme, but written in different form.

Nº 16 - Starts with half notes and rests. Observe the repeat (:‖) marks at the end of each lesson, indicating that it must be played twice.

Nº 17 - Contains quarters, half notes and rests.

Nº 18 - Contains dotted half notes. The dot contains half the value of the note which precedes it, giving the first note E the value of three beats.

Observe the slur in this lesson. The note G on the fourth beat is tied by a slur to the first note, meaning that the air should not be interrupted by the tongue. Attack the first note with a T, move the fingers softly to reach the note C in the next bar, which is again attacked with a T.

Nº 19 - Here the slur is extended, reaching over to the second bar. Attack the first note, moving the fingers softly and evenly again. Tie the five notes together as if they were only one.

Nº 20 - The Syncope is here introduced. Syncopation is also called Rag-time. It occurs when music is written against the regular time, or when the weak beat is tied to the strong beat. In 4/4 time, the first and third are the strong, and the second and fourth are the weak beats. In this lesson you will see that the second, or weak beat is tied to the third or strong, and the fourth or weak is tied to the first beat in the next bar, which makes that part syncopated. Attack first, second and third note, the last to be held over to the next bar, playing the two Cs as if they were one, giving them the value of two beats as you would for the second note G.

Nº 21 - Here you will notice that the first note E has the value of two beats and is followed by four eighth notes, which together must be given the same value as the E. This group of four notes has the time value of a half note. Attack the first and second notes. In the thirteenth, fourteenth and fifteenth bars, only the first note is tongued.

Nos. 22 & 23 - The slur appears here in different lengths. Observe them carefully.

Nº 24 - Here, dotted eighths followed by sixteenth notes are introduced. The dotted eighth must be given three times the value of the following sixteenth note. In observing this, try to avoid the following mistake which is very frequently made by careless musicians.

Thus: changing similar pasages from common 4/4 into 12/8 time.

Attack every note clearly.

Nº 25 - This is a syncopated lesson. Starting with an eighth note followed by quarter notes indicates that the second, third fourth and fifth notes must be attacked in the middle of the first, second, third and fourth beats respectively.

The following example is identical with the first two bars:

Nº 26 - This lesson is based on playing, what is generally called, after-beats. The lesson starts with an eighth rest, starting the first note on the second half of the first beat. The pupil who is apt to become confused with the rests and the correct time to attack, might refer to the following example and count eighths which will simplify the counting.

Notice that this bar contains eight eighths, so instead of counting four, count eight, doubling the time. This would give one count to each figure.

Nº 27 - Attack first, third and fourth note of each group. The second is tied to the first.

The dots above the notes indicate that they should be played with a short stroke of the tongue. (Staccato)

Nº 28 - Attack first, second and third note of each group. First and second staccato, the fourth is tied to the third.

Nº 29 - Attack first and third of each group.

Nº 30 - Attack first, second, fourth, sixth and eighth notes, slur others.

Nº 31 - Attack first and fourth notes in each group. Fourth and eighth staccato.

Nº 32 - Attack first and second in each group. First and fifth staccato.

Nº 33 - This lesson is in the form of a schottische or Fox Trot. The line through the ¢ indicates that the 4/4 or common time is cut in half. Thus this lesson is played in 2/4 time. The Schottische or Fox Trot tempo is rather slow 2/4 or fast 4/4 (¢).

Play this lesson as if it were written like this:

in slow tempo.

Nº 34 - This lesson is written in waltz time (3/4). Three rather fast beats to the bar or one slow beat to the bar.

Nº 35 - Here the theme has taken the form of a Mazurka or three-step. The Mazurka tempo is much slower than that of the waltz.

Progressive exercises on articulation

24

Thirty-Sixth Lesson
MAJOR SCALES AND THEIR RELATIVE MINORS

Here are the scales in all the different keys.

To find the relative minor to any major scale, count one and a half tones or a minor third lower than the key note. The signatures of both the major and its relative minor are the same.

The difference between a major and a minor scale is found in its degrees.

It has already been stated that the major scale consists of five whole and two semitones, or half tones. The half tones are between the third and fourth, and between the seventh and eighth degrees ascending or descending.

There are two kinds of minor scales, Melodic and Harmonic. The melodic is shown in the illustration. We will not go into detail regarding the Harmonic at this time. It has three half tones, which come between the second and third, fifth and sixth, and the seventh and eighth degrees. This makes an interval of a tone and a half between the sixth and seventh degrees. The Harmonic Minor scale is the same in ascending and descending.

In the Melodic Minor scale there are six whole and two semi-tones, but these are placed in different positions. The first half tone is between the second and third, and the second between the seventh and eighth in ascending. In descending, the first half tone comes between the third and fourth and the second stays in its place between the sixth and seventh notes.

In the Melodic Minor scale in ascending, the sixth and seventh notes are raised a half tone, while in descending the same two notes are lowered again to their natural pitch. "See example."

The student should learn all the Major and Minor scales so that he can play them from memory.

36th Lesson
MAJOR SCALES AND THEIR RELATIVE MINORS

A major

F# minor

E major

C# minor

B major

G# minor

F# major

Bb major

G minor

Eb major

C minor

Ab major

F minor

Twenty Easy Recreations

MELODY

PRELUDE

DIVERSION

CANTABILE

MARCH

POLKA

TWO-STEP

ANDANTE

ARIA

SCHOTTISCHE

MAZURKA

TYROLIEN

WALTZ

WALTZ

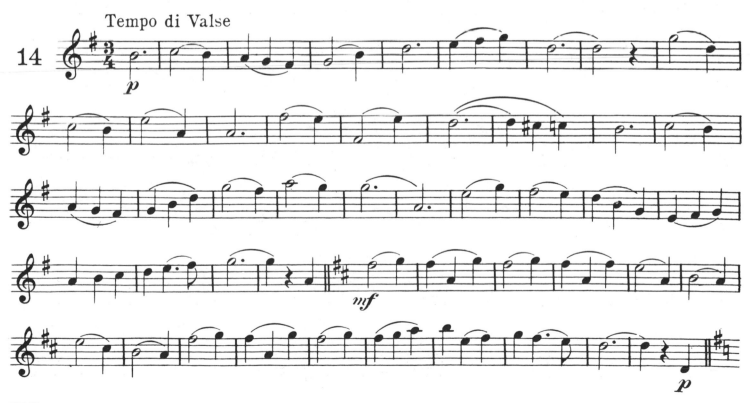

Trio

QUADRILLE

Allegro moderato

15

Trio

D.C.

TWO-STEP

16

INDIAN SKETCH

17

POLKA

18

D.C.

FOX-TROT

Moderato

19

D.C.

GAVOTTE

20

D.C. al 𝄐

THE GRUPETTO

The Grupetto (or Turn) is indicated thus: (∽). It consists of four little grace notes. Sometimes these notes are written in the music and at other times they are only designated by the sign. The sign is placed either over or after a principal note.

The value of the Grupetto is taken from the note preceding it, not from the note following. It consists of four notes viz: that on the degree above, then the degree of the principal note, then that of the degree below, which in most cases is a half tone, and lastly again that of the principal note.

When a sharp is placed under a turn, the lowest note of the group must be made sharp. When a flat is placed above a turn, the highest note must be made flat.

If there are no accidentals marked over or under the turn, both the upper and lower notes must be played in accordance with the key signature.

The Grupetto is purely ornamental and should therefore be played smoothly and gracefully. The Grupetto is sometimes composed of three, five and six notes. In such instances, the music is generally completely written out, so that no sign is necessary.

The Grupetto may also be inverted thus: (∾) In this case the first note of the group is on the degree below the principal note, the second the principal, the third the one above the principal and the fourth again the principal note.

Rienzi, by Richard Wagner.

Example as written

as played

It should be noticed that the Grupetto is always tied to the note preceding it except if otherwise indicated.

Nº 1.   These Grupettos are written in their natural key signature.

Nº 2.   Grupettos with all their signatures.

Nº 3.   The natural (♮) mark below or above a Grupetto indicates that while the motive is written either in flats or sharps, the higher or lower note must be played natural.

Nº 4.   Andante, in which the Grupette appears in a different form.

The Grupetto

THE TRILL.

The Trill (or shake) marked thus: "*tr·*" or "*tr*~~~~", consists of a rapid alternation of the note so marked with the note on the next degree above it.

A trill as a rule, is ended with an appoggiatura, a turn or some other grace notes, which are generally indicated in the notation.

The trill must be carefully practised. If a long trill is to be made, start it rather slowly, with an increasing velocity.

The trill generally ends with two grace notes which must be played smoothly. The last notes of the trill may decrease slightly in velocity so as to make a gracefull and pleasing finish.

The duration of the trill is always the same as the value given to the note. The trill extends sometimes through several bars. In this case the sign "*tr*" is given an extension thus:

The Andante Moderato must be carefully played, observing all the marks.

At the end of this lesson A♭ is trilled with B♭. This can be easily accomplished by holding the A♭ key open while trilling with the B♭ key. (VI)

The trill from C to D is simplified by holding C, 2nd finger on pad B, and trilling the D with key VIII.

The Trill

As written

As played

Andante moderato

p

cres _ cen _ _ do   f

f

accel.   ff   rall.

a tempo

Exercises on Scales in Thirds
(COMPRISING ALL KEY'S)

B minor

G major

E minor

C major

Exercises on Chromatic Scales

Difficult Passages
(SIMPLIFIED BY THE ADOPTION OF EXTRA KEYS)

Nº 1. For the use of the extra B♭ key. (or A♯)
Keep first finger of the right hand down. (See Key D in Chart)

Nº 2. For the use of the extra E♭. (D♯)
To be taken with the middle finger of right hand. (Pad E in Chart)

No. 3. For the use of the extra A♭ (G♯)
        Keep little finger of left hand down (Key V in Chart)

No. 4. For the use of the extra G♭ (F♯)
        Taken with the third finger of right hand (Key XIII in Chart)

Keep 2nd finger of right hand open.......   Take D♯ with middle finger...........

No. 5. Simplified by the Single octave key System.

Nº 6. A third B♭ key is found on some instruments and placed so that it can be used with second finger of the left hand. It helps considerably in passages like the following, (A♭⁻ᵇⁱˢ in Chart)

(Use third finger on second, and little finger on third finger plate)

Nº 7. The high E and F are difficult keys to manipulate, but with the extra key for these, passages like the following can be executed with more ease and accuracy.

(This key is taken with first finger of the left hand) which is placed above the A pad

Nº 8. This exercise can be played with key V open

(Manipulated with little finger of the left hand)

54

Exercises for the Saxophone

having the three Petals for the lower register,
which are manipulated with the middle finger
of right hand

(Evette and Schaeffer System)

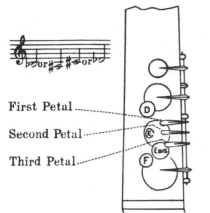

First Petal

Second Petal

Third Petal

A♯(or B♭) Produced with the aid of first Petal.

C♯(or D♭) Produced with the aid of third Petal.

D♭ with third Petal.   C♯ and A♯ with third and first Petal.

B♮ with second Petal.   B♮ and C♯ with second and third Petal.

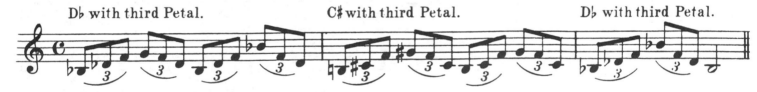

D♭ with third Petal.   C♯ with third Petal.   D♭ with third Petal.

C♯ with third Petal. Keep little finger of left hand on key V.

Exercises for the E♭,(or D♯)

To produce E♭ take pad E♭is with second finger
of right hand

(Evette and Schaeffer System)

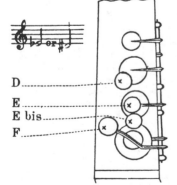

D

E

E bis

F

Keep A♭ open   Keep D♭ Key open

Keep A♭ open

19911-102

№ 13 Exercise for the use of All Extra Keys

Exercises on All Perfect Chords

USE THE EXTRA KEYS AT EVERY OPPORTUNITY

C# minor

A major

F# minor

D major

B minor

G major

E minor

C major

Exercises on the Dominant Seventh

Exercises on the Diminished Seventh

C major

A minor

F major

D minor

14 Solos by Celebrated Composers
Cradle Song
(Chant de Berceau)

M. HAUSER

Berceuse

F. RENARD

Ave Maria
(Adapted from Bach's 1st Prelude)

CHARLES GOUNOD

Träumerei and Romance

ROBERT SCHUMANN

Intermezzo
(Cavalleria Rusticana)

PIETRO MASCAGNI

The Secret
Intermezzo

L. GAUTIER
Transcribed by Ben Vereecken

Trio

La Cinquantaine
(The Golden Wedding)

GABRIEL P. MARIE
Transcribed by Ben Vereecken

Simple Confession
(Simple Aveu)

FRANCIS THOME

Largo

GEORG FRIEDRICH HÄNDEL
Transcribed by Ben Vereecken

Serenade
(Ständchen)

FRANZ SCHUBERT

Spring Song
(Frühlingslied)

FELIX MENDELSSOHN-BARTHOLDY

Allegretto grazioso

11

Sextet

from

"Lucia di Lammermoor"

GAETANO DONIZETTI
Transcribed by Ben Vereecken

Copyright MCMXXIX by Carl Fischer Inc., New York
International Copyright Secured

Angel's Serenade
(La Serenata)

GAETANO BRAGA
Transcribed by Ben Vereecken

Andante con moto

13

Copyright MCMXXIX by Carl Fischer Inc New York
International Copyright Secured

Nocturne

FREDERIC F. CHOPIN

Fifty Progressive Exercises in Prelude Form

Love's Declaration
Cavatine
Four Solos
Especially written for this Method by the Author

Don Gonzales
Bolero (Caprice)

Youthfulness
Fantasie

Grand Caprice
Introduction, Theme, Variations and Finale

Introduction
Maestoso

Adagio

Tutti

Andante cantabile

Andantino

A LIST OF THE PRINCIPAL WORDS USED IN MODERN MUSIC.

WITH THEIR ABBREVIATIONS AND EXPLANATIONS.

A................to, in, or at; *A tempo*, in time.
Accelerando (*accel.*).....Gradually increasing the speed.
Accent................Emphasis on certain parts of the measure.
Adagio................Slow; leisurely.
Ad libitum (*ad lib.*)....At pleasure; not in strict time.
A due (*a 2*)...........To be played by both instruments.
Agitato................Restless, with agitation.
Al or Alla................In the style of.
Alla Marcia................In the style of a March.
Allegretto................Moderately quick.
Allegro................Quick and lively.
Allegro assai................Very rapidly.
Amore................Love. *Con amore*, Fondly; tenderly.
Amoroso................Affectionately.
Andante................In moderately slow time.
Andantino................A little less slow than Andante.
Anima, con }
Animato } ....With animation.
A piacere................At pleasure.
Appassionato................Impassioned.
Arpeggio................A broken chord.
Assai................Very: *Allegro assai*, very rapidly.
A tempo................In the original movement.
Attacca................Commence the next movement at once.
Barcarolle................A Venetian boatman's song.
Ben................Well; *Ben marcato*, well marked.
Bis................Twice; repeat the passage.
Bravura................Brilliant, bold, spirited.
Brillante................Showy, sparkling, brilliant.
Brio, con................With much spirit.
Cadenza................A passage introduced as an embellishment.
Calando................Decreasing in power and speed.
Cantabile................In a singing style.
Caprice................A composition of irregular construction.
Capriccio, a................At pleasure.
Cavatina................A movement in vocal style. [sounds.
Chord................A combination of three or more musical
Coda................A finishing movement.
Col or con................With.
Crescendo (*cres.*)........Gradually louder.
Da or dal................From.
Da Capo (*D. C.*)........From the beginning.
Dal Segno (*D. S.*)........From the sign.
Decrescendo (*decresc.*)..Decreasing in strength.
Delicatezza, con........Delicately; refined in style.
Diminuendo (*dim.*).....Gradually softer.
Divisi................Divided. Each part to be played by a sepa-
Dolce................Softly, sweetly. [rate instrument.
Dolcissimo................Very sweetly and softly.
Dominant................The fifth tone in the major or minor scale.
Duet or duo................A composition for two performers.
E................And.
Elegante................Elegant; graceful.
Embouchure................The mouthpiece of a wind instrument.
Enharmonic................Alike in pitch but different in notation.
Energico................With energy, vigorously.
Espressione, con........Expressively, with expression.
Finale................The concluding movement.
Fine................The end.
Forte (*f*)................Loud.
Forte-piano (*fp*)........Loud and instantly soft again.
Fortissimo (*ff*)........Very loud.
Forza................Force of tone.
Forzando (*fz*)........Accentuate the sound.
Fuoco, con................With fire; with spirit.
Furioso................Furiously; passionately.
Giocoso................Joyously; playfully.
Giusto................Exact; in strict time.
Grandioso................Grand; pompous; majestic.
Grave................Very slow and solemn.
Grazioso................Gracefully.
Gusto................Taste.
Harmony................A combination of musical sounds.
Key-note................The first degree of the Scale.
Largamente................Very broad in style.
Larghetto................Slow, but not so slow as Largo.
Largo................Broad and slow.
Legato................Smoothly, the reverse of Staccato.
Leger-line................A small added line above or below the staff.
Leggiero................Lightly.
Lento................Slow, but not as slow as Largo.
L'istesso tempo........In the same time.
Loco................Play as written, no longer 8va.
Ma................But. *Ma non troppo*, But not too much.
Maestoso................Majestically, dignified.
Maggiore................Major Key.
Marcato................**Marked. With distinctness and emphasis.**

Meno................Less. *Meno mosso*, Less quickly.
Mezzo................Moderately.
Mezzo piano (*mp*).....Moderately soft.
Mindre................Minor Key.
Moderato................Moderately. *Allegro moderato*, moderately
Molto................Much; very. [fast.
Morendo................Gradually softer.
Mosso................Moved. *Piu mosso*, quicker.
Moto................Motion. *Con moto*, with animation.
Non................Not.
Notation................{ The art of representing musical sounds
................{ by characters visible to the eye.
Obligato................An indispensable part.
Octave................A series of 8 consecutive diatonic tones.
Opus (*Op.*)................A work.
Ossia................Or; or else. Generally indicating an easier
Ottava (*8va*)................To be played an octave higher. [method.
Pause (⌒)................The sign indicating pause or finish.
Perdendosi................Dying away gradually.
Pesante................Heavily; with firm and vigorous execution.
Piacere, a................At pleasure.
Pianissimo (*pp*)........Very soft.
Piano (*p*)................Soft.
Piu................More. *Piu Allegro*, More quickly.
Poco or un poco................A little.
Poco a poco................Gradually, by degrees.
Poco piu mosso................A little faster.
Poco meno................A little slower.
Poco piu................A little faster.
Poi................Then; afterwards.
Pomposo................Pompous, grand.
Prestissimo................As fast as possible.
Presto................Very quick; faster than Allegro.
Primo (*1mo*)................The first.
Quartet................A piece of music for four performers.
Quasi................As if; similar to; in the style of.
Quintet................A piece of music for five performers.
Rallentando (*rall.*)......Gradually slower.
Rinforzando................With special emphasis.
Ritardando (*rit.*)........Slackening speed.
Risoluto................Resolutely; bold; energetic.
Ritenuto................Retarding the time.
Scherzando................Playfully; sportively.
Secondo (*2do*)................The second time (or part.)
Seconda volta................The second time.
Segue................Follow on in similar style.
Semplice................Simply; unaffectedly.
Sempre................Always; continually.
Senza................Without. *Senza sordino*, Without mute.
Sforzando (*sf*)........Forcibly; with sudden emphasis.
Simile................In like manner.
Smorzando (*smorz.*)....Diminishing the sound.
Solo................For one performer only.
Sordino................A Mute. *Con Sordino*, With the Mute.
Sostenuto................Sustained, prolonged.
Sotto................Under. *Sotto voce*, In a subdued tone.
Spirito................Spirit. *Con Spirito*, Forcefully.
Staccato................Detached, separated.
Stentando................Dragging or retarding the tempo.
Stretto................An increase of speed. *Piu Stretto*, Faster.
Subdominant................The 4th tone in the diatonic scale.
Syncopation................Change of accent from a strong beat to a
Tacet................Be silent. [weak one.
Tempo................Movement.
Tempo primo................As at first.
Tenuto (*ten.*)................Held for the full value.
Theme................The subject or melody.
Timbre................Quality of tone.
Tonic................The key-note of any scale.
Tremolo................A trembling, fluttering movement.
Trio................A piece of music for three performers.
Triplet................{ A group of 3 notes to be performed in the
................{ time of two of equal value.
Troppo................Too much. *Allegro ma non troppo*, not too
Tutti................All; all the instruments. [quick.
Un................A; one; an.
Unison................Alike in pitch.
Una corda................On one string.
Variation................The transformation and embellishment of a
Veloce................Rapid; swift; quick. [melody.
Vibrato................A wavy tone-effect which should be sparing-
Vivace................With vivacity; bright; spirited. [ly used.
Vivo................Lively.
Voce................The voice; a certain part.
Volkslied................A national or folk song.
Volti subito (*V. S.*).....Turn over quickly.